MW01259798

My Rosary
Coloring and Activity Book

Written and illustrated by
Virginia Helen Richards, FSP
and D. Thomas Halpin, FSP

Pauline
BOOKS & MEDIA

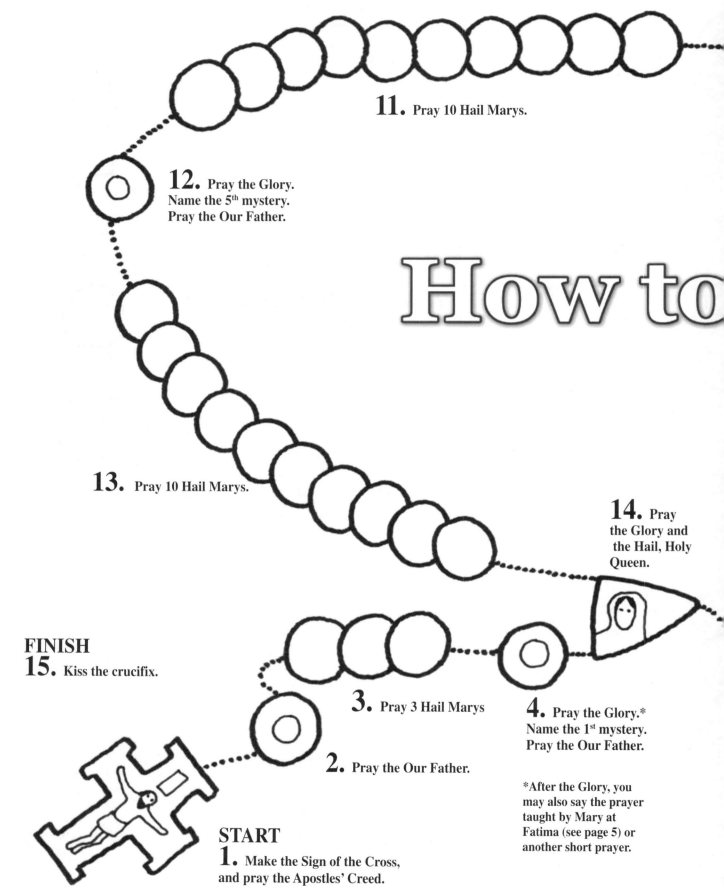

11. Pray 10 Hail Marys.

12. Pray the Glory.
Name the 5th mystery.
Pray the Our Father.

How to

13. Pray 10 Hail Marys.

14. Pray
the Glory and
the Hail, Holy
Queen.

FINISH
15. Kiss the crucifix.

3. Pray 3 Hail Marys

4. Pray the Glory.*
Name the 1st mystery.
Pray the Our Father.

2. Pray the Our Father.

*After the Glory, you
may also say the prayer
taught by Mary at
Fatima (see page 5) or
another short prayer.

START
1. Make the Sign of the Cross,
and pray the Apostles' Creed.

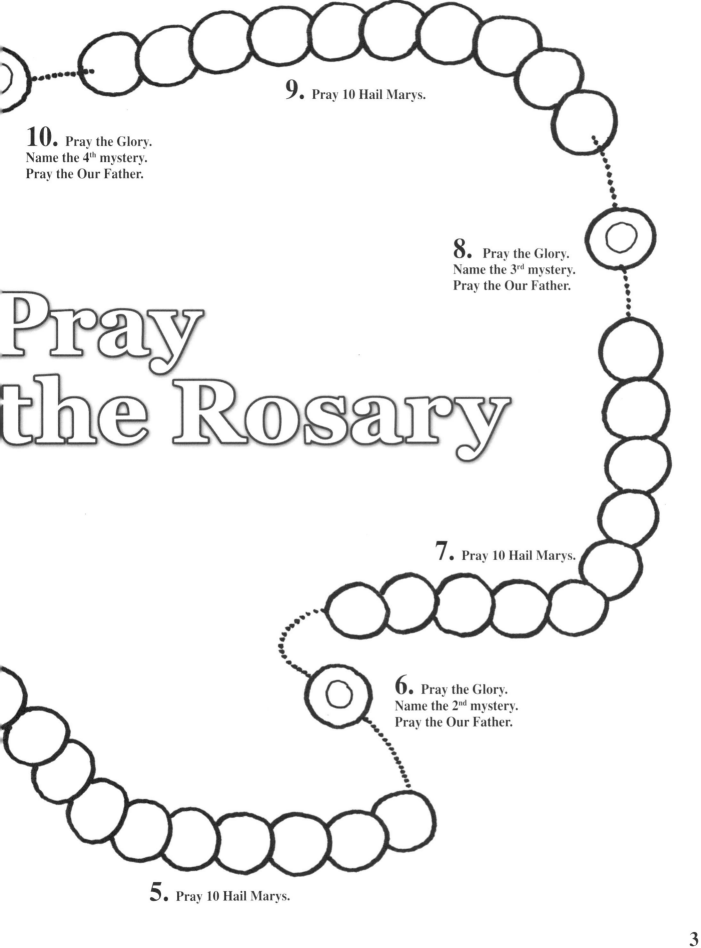

9. Pray 10 Hail Marys.

10. Pray the Glory.
Name the 4th mystery.
Pray the Our Father.

8. Pray the Glory.
Name the 3rd mystery.
Pray the Our Father.

Pray the Rosary

7. Pray 10 Hail Marys.

6. Pray the Glory.
Name the 2nd mystery.
Pray the Our Father.

5. Pray 10 Hail Marys.

The Prayers We Say in the Rosary

The Sign of the Cross

In the name of the Father, and of the Son, and of the Holy Spirit. Amen.

Our Father

Our Father, who art in heaven, hallowed be thy name. Thy kingdom come. Thy will be done on earth as it is in heaven. Give us this day our daily bread, and forgive us our trespasses, as we forgive those who trespass against us. And lead us not into temptation; but deliver us from evil. Amen.

Hail Mary

Hail Mary, full of grace, the Lord is with you. Blessed are you among women and blessed is the fruit of your womb, Jesus. Holy Mary, Mother of God, pray for us sinners, now and at the hour of our death. Amen.

Glory

Glory to the Father, and to the Son, and to the Holy Spirit: as it was in the beginning, is now, and will be for ever. Amen.

Hail, Holy Queen

Hail, holy Queen, Mother of Mercy, our life, our sweetness, and our hope. To you do we cry, poor banished children of Eve; to you do we send up our sighs, mourning and weeping in this valley of tears. Turn then, most gracious advocate, your eyes of mercy toward us, and after this our exile, show unto us the blessed fruit of your womb, Jesus. O clement, O loving, O sweet Virgin Mary.

The Fatima Decade Prayer

O my Jesus, forgive us our sins, save us from the fires of hell. Lead all souls to heaven, especially those most in need of your mercy.

The Apostles' Creed

I believe in God, the Father almighty,

creator of heaven and earth.

I believe in Jesus Christ, his only Son, our Lord.

He was conceived by the power of the Holy Spirit

and born of the Virgin Mary.

He suffered under Pontius Pilate,

was crucified, died and was buried.

He descended to the dead.

On the third day he rose again.

He ascended into heaven,

and is seated at the right hand of the Father.

He will come again to judge the living and the dead.

I believe in the Holy Spirit,

the holy catholic Church,

the communion of saints,

the forgiveness of sins,

the resurrection of the body,

and the life everlasting.

Amen.

1st **Joyful Mystery:** Mary becomes God's Mother

The angel Gabriel tells Mary that God has chosen her to be the mother of his Son. Mary says, "Yes, I will!" **Mary, help me to do what God wants.**

2nd **Joyful Mystery:** Mary visits St. Elizabeth

Mary visits and helps St. Elizabeth. **Mary, help me to be loving and kind.**

3rd Joyful Mystery: Jesus is born

Jesus is born in Bethlehem. Mary and Joseph care for him. **Mary, help me to love Jesus always.**

4ᵗʰ **Joyful Mystery:** Jesus is presented in the Temple

Mary and Joseph bring Jesus to the Temple. **Thank you, Heavenly Father, for sending us Jesus our Savior!**

5th **Joyful Mystery:** Jesus is found in the Temple

When Mary and Joseph find Jesus in the Temple talking about God, they take Jesus home. **Jesus, help me obey at home and at school.**

1ˢᵗ Mystery of Light: John baptizes Jesus

John baptizes Jesus in the Jordan River. **Jesus, help me to live as a child of God.**

2nd **Mystery of Light:** Jesus works his first miracle

Jesus turns water into wine at a wedding party in Cana. **Jesus, I believe you are truly God!**

3rd **Mystery of Light:** Jesus preaches to the crowds

Jesus teaches people about the Kingdom of God. **Jesus, help me to listen when you speak to me in my heart.**

4ᵗʰ **Mystery of Light:** Jesus is transfigured

Three of the apostles see Jesus shining with God's glory on Mount Tabor. Moses and Elijah are with him. **Jesus, I want to love you always.**

5th **Mystery of Light:** Jesus gives us the Holy Eucharist

Before he dies Jesus gives us his Body and his Blood—a great mystery!
Jesus, help me to love and treasure you in the Eucharist.

1st Sorrowful Mystery: Jesus prays in the garden

Jesus knows that he is about to die. He prays to be strong. **Jesus, help me when I'm sad or afraid.**